Autumn Blush

A Collection of Poetry

by *Michael Hanson*

YaYe Books
Colorado

Autumn Blush: A Collection of Poetry
Copyright © 2007 YaYe Books

All rights reserved. No part of this book may be reproduced in any manner whatsoever without prior written permission from the publisher, except where noted in the text and in the case of brief quotations embodied in critical articles and reviews.

Visit our Web site: www.yayedesign.com

Credits
Cover and interior design: Helen H. Harrison
Cover painting reproduced by permission of Cedric Egeli

Library of Congress Control Number: 2007938697
ISBN 978-0-9798652-4-4

10 9 8 7 6 5 4 3 2 1   15 14 13 12 11 10 09 08 07 06
Printed in the United States of America.

Dedicated to
the memory of

Martita Aldea Casey Hanson

my Mother

Acknowledgments

The following people were instrumental in the evolution of this anthology:

Graphic Artist and big sister Helen Harrison for the inspired cover and interior designs as well as all text formatting; big brother Keith Hanson for his kind words to a 15-year-old wannabe-poet some years ago; my other big brother Wayne Hanson and my little sister Cindy Adler for their love and fellowship across the seasons; sister-in-law and confidante Terry Hanson for taking the author photographs (with the able assistance of my nephew Jeffrey) and for electronically archiving many of my early drafts; Screenplay-Collaborator and good friend Ralph Coviello, and Sci-Fi/Fantasy Author Arthur Sanchez, for their insightful advice that I start engaging in public poetry readings; DVD Producer and fellow S.U. Grad Chris Chaplin for insisting that I save and compile my writings; California Author Lynda Foley for pushing me to cut my own path in the world of literature; longtime Correspondent Jaime Halbert for her eternal optimism; Digital Artist Lee Ann Kuruganti for her spot-on literary assessments; Small Press Publisher Jean Goldstrom for convincing me that a collection of my poetry was a viable prospect; fellow New Jersyan Mary Miller for guiding me to the world of online publishing; fellow IEEE Staff Editor Margie Rafferty for proofreading the galleys; and renowned Maryland Portrait Artists Cedric and Joanette Egeli for encouraging my lyrical aspirations and for allowing a digital sampling of Cedric's beautiful painting of Plein Air Artist, Sarah Wardell.

From the depth of my soul, I thank you all.

Michael Hanson
Piscataway, NJ
Fall 2007

Contents

Autumn Woman   7
Climb   8
I Dream Of Eire   9
Wander   10
The Edge   11
Second Love   12
Paper Wings   13
On Lonely Days   14
Alone   15
Mountain Sea   16
Dog And   17
Cat And   18
Charlemagne   19
Falls   20
Within Her Eyes   21
I Dream Of You   22
Moment   23
Enchanting Me   24
Within Her Smile   25
Yes She Loves   26
Sarah Dances   27
Your Smile In Me   28
With My Eyes   29
When Sarah Dreams   30
To Know You   31
The Locks Of Night   32
Haunting Me   33
Adirondac Eulogy   34
Mother Ghost   35

Three Promises   36
Fusilier   37
Beyond These Walls   39
Of Another   40
Annalee   41
Cannoneer   43
Aunjanu   45
Fear   47
All Hallow's Eve   48
Cape's End   49
Furnace   50
Furled Wings   51
Harbor Night   52
Is Still   53
Provincetown   54
Remember Thee   55
Autumn   56
Autumn Stroll   57
Autumn Blush   58
Grove Troopers   59
November Dreams   60
November   61
Winter Tears   63
Winter Bride   64
Ice Maiden   65
April's Reign   66
Spring   67
Summertime   69
Summer's Breath   70
Precious Petals   71
Sirens   72

Autumn Woman

She floats beside a chastened tree
astir upon the cusp of night
to bathe in summer's fading breeze
and dress 'neath sweetened amber light.

She walks upon this twilight land
where rising sun meets falling star
a timeless tryst older than man
a naked dance of ancient charms.

Until she spies the boundary
of cold denial held at bay
and roughly shorn of golden sleep
she wakes to bear another day.

And bravely unrepentant screams
demand the truths of all her dreams.

Climb

Upon a mountain path I paused
mid helpless base and wizened peak
to realize I had no cause,
nor brave crusade, nor mighty feat,

And glancing down upon this trail
I saw no tolls or rough blockades
no dreams composing brilliant tales
a simply traveled gentle way.

And looking up I shed a tear
and pondered my remaining climb
and lurking unexpected fears
and dark detours comprising time.

And in that naked moment bow'd
upon this hike so poorly spent
I made this frank yet humble vow
to conquer harsher grand ascents.

I Dream of Eire

On starry nights I dream of Eire
and faded paths and sunny strolls
and wafts of heather scented air
and verdant fields that stir my soul.

Fair Dublin I would roam awhile
in Temple Bar's sweet smoky lairs
and just to see a shy lass smile
I'd compliment her fiery hair.

I'd hear the pipes of Uilleann
herald silver songs of joy
as Irish harpers join the din
and dance of Gaelic girls and boys.

I'd walk the streets of Dingle town
on cobblestones past green shop doors
and wander out across the downs
to standing stones that guard the shore.

Of Eire I dream beneath the stars
fair emerald daughter of the sea
this distant son of Celtic charms
still faithful to the land of Sidhe.

Wander

I wander through an Autumn pale
to ponder joyous bluebird songs
as piles of gathered leaves exhale
sweet perfumes only fires spawn.

And walking through this heady bog
I flirt with all the supple trees
that sway in swirls of morning fog
with grassy skirts upon their knees.

And fancying a laughing brook
whose freshest kiss is wet and cool
I'm captured by her sultry looks
until I spot another jewel.

A saucy bold sashaying trail
whose naughty turns are fey and fun
escorts me to a shadowed vale
from whence my journey had begun.

Beside a lake I reach the end
and cabin that I call my home
that sits within a silent glen
companionless and all alone.

The Edge

One day I came upon a shore
where stable land meets stormy sea
deciding that I wanted more
from life than pale reality.

And standing at the ocean's lee
I fumbled on wet shifting sands
that mark the final boundary
and mere existence of a man.

And hesitating on that shoal
I pondered what my life deserved
and found my meal an empty bowl
of feasts that I was never served.

Then taking in the full expanse
of rough untested waters near
I realized my final chance
to conquer all my lasting fears.

And stumbling like a yearling child
I plunged chaotic and amazed
and laughing curses fey and wild
I dove into dark unknown waves.

Second Love

Beyond first love a chasm yawns
'Tween Autumn's death and April joy
From whence the lonely dread the dawn
As shattered hearts like broken toys
Will contemplate a union gone
Twixt tempered souls sublimely coy.

In depths perceived unlimited
Inside a house of silent doors
A sad and empty marriage bed
Sits innocent and unexplored
A testament of passion fled
A tome of melancholy lore.

Within the depths of tragic loss
Upon the heights of wounded peace
A hurt expresses painful cost
With cold regret a bitter feast
'Til skins of shame are shed and tossed
And second love at last released.

Paper Wings

I soar upon the very dreams
and errant wisps of daily pause
that mark the breadth and boundary
of my imagination's cause.

I dip and glide amidst the shapes
of all my favored darling days
inhabiting this bright landscape
enrapt within its loving gaze.

'Til tripping I begin my fall
and fading muses sadly sing
that I am just a simple soul
with feet of clay and paper wings.

On Lonely Days

On lonely days I wander here
far from glass and steel and stone
beyond the reach of crowded fear
where all my thoughts can stand alone.

I rest my soul in solitude
free of life's enduring pains
securely gripped with fortitude
in arms that soothe away all blame.

And when my jaunt has reached its end
and duty wakes me to the lie
I leave this favored ancient den
and bid my secret place goodbye.

Alone

An ashen sky 'twixt night and day
a soulless land of dust and stone
an endless path of level grey
an empty silent hollow home.

Where loving smiles are mythic dreams
and laughter is an ancient song
canards of aging cryptic creeds
lamenting all enduring wrongs.

Thus echoes never wander here
and colors surely never grow
inside this skin of doubt and fear
the doom and curse of life...alone.

Mountain Sea

Amidst your heights of frosted air
among majestic rocky peaks
and oceanside my leafy lair
a garden lush verdant valley.

So far apart our simple homes
dividing us by space and time
yet still we know we're not alone
and that we hear each other's cries.

Two distant songs of faded strain
two dreams caressing in the night
a couplet edited in twain
a haunting geographic plight.

Joined, but separate, you and me
upon your mountain in my sea.

Dog and

Dog and child forever wild
communicating without words
hand and paw unduly riled
the playful mix of kid and cur.

Dog and boy in search of joy
will rollick 'cross the countryside
swift and sure and ever coy
eternities to chase and hide.

Dog and man upon the sand
a ritual and honored bond
six limbs trodding changeless land
a link across millennium.

Two as one inseparable fun
an ancient hallowed union.

Cat and

Cat and child forever wild
with dangling strings and catnip toys
hand and paw unduly riled
the playful land of kitten joys.

Cat and girl alive awhirl
will spring and laugh and dance and bounce
swift and sure with glee unfurled
eternitys to stalk and pounce.

Cat and woman 'neath the sun
a ritual and honored bond
six limbs pacing, races done
a link across millennium.

Two as one inseparable fun
an ancient hallowed union.

Charlemagne

The prince of cats came wandering
with orange, blue, and white his mane
this foundling fierce and sauntering
this calico named Charlemagne.

Alone of manly whiskered kind
most singular of coat and sock
no brothers of the race feline
a cat apart upon this walk.

"Does not exist!" says humankind.
"Anomaly!" their vile taunt.
But caring not for words that bind
brave Charlemagne enjoys his jaunt.

Fair noble colors chest and brow
forever lonely, always proud.

Falls

Whence on a distant northern trek
within sweet Summer's final breath
I came unto this fabled neck
a mighty thund'ring gorge of death.

Its underestimated rage
its harsh and powerful allure
its vaunted volume never gauged
its overwhelming frank furor.

A pilgrim down upon its feet
baptized in pounding icy rain
I drown in mortal man's defeat
to nature's grand majestic fame.

An ancient testament to strife
this rumbling spectacle of life.

Within Her Eyes

Within her eyes I see my heart
which sings a rage inside my chest
a savage feral song a part
of all the love I can't express.

Within her eyes I lose myself
and drown in pools of tender bliss
my incoherent pleas a knell
for want of one sweet precious kiss.

Within her eyes my need sets fire
a passion I cannot contain
a holocaust of deep desire
and feelings that will never wane.

And in the depths within her eyes
I breathe a thousand blessed sighs.

I Dream of You

I dream of you on restless eves
when loneliness becomes a fire
amidst sweet blazing orchard trees
we taste the fruit of strong desire.

I dream of you upon the shore
in crashing surf and ocean spray
as laughter drowns within the roar
and water carries us away.

I dream of you within my arms
a treasure soft and eloquent
a smile imbued with golden charms
and kisses I have never spent.

And thus denying waking truth
I dream and dream and dream of you.

Moment

For a breath I then appear
between the fading light
a wicked grin upon the shade
a quick and silver sprite.

And in the blink of your dark eyes
a gesture almost missed
our noses touch in brief respite
and I give you a kiss.

Your gasp of sudden sweet surprise
a nectar of delight
that sends me on my merry way
to whisper in the night.

Enchanting Me

Annointed in fair Summer's gown
upon an effervescent beach
'neath azure tinted silver down
I find your face enchanting me.

Your grin a string of pearls so bright
reflecting oceanic gleams
your guise a vision of delight
with haunting smile enchanting me.

Your gentle arms enwrap my soul
with passion tendered lovingly
fey spirit that I fear to hold
with lovely eyes enchanting me.

Embraced in honeyed harmony
enraptured most enchantingly.

Within Her Smile

Within her smile a soul imbued
with glowing dreams and tender grace
thus paints a heart's eternal feud
upon her gentle loving face.

Within her smile a subtle frown
a song inscribed in ancient lore
with saddened eyes of deepest brown
that melt into my very core.

Within her smile a fruit so sweet
it culls me as a fickle cad
and drags me down unto her feet
to grovel like a common lad.

And humbled now without my guile
I worship thus within her smile

Yes She Loves

Yes she loves the break of day
and soothing Summer light,
she loves the bluejay's crystal song,
she loves the covers tight.

She loves the thrill of light blue skies
and air that's sweet and fresh,
she loves the richness of the trees,
she loves the sound of "yes."

She loves the taste of spicy food
the company of friends,
she loves the magic of the night,
she loves to make amends.

She loves the thrill of starlit walks,
she loves the sounds of toys,
she loves what fate has given her,
the hurts as well as joys.

She sees her very life is art
expressed within a poem,
this song which treasures all her heart
oh blessed lovely soul.

Sarah Dances

Sarah dances with the Moon
embraced in milky twilight arms
free of life's enduring brace
enchanted by an ancient charm.

Gaudy heavens shine above
as both her sparkling eyes ignite
and with the birth of her bright smile
her silver lover stills the night.

And as these two fey spirits laugh
and splash in lakes of starlit glee
Sarah wakes from her sweet dream
a healed and reborn refugee.

Your Smile in Me

I carry your smile in me
safe inside, and everywhere
I go not alone you see
my darling, without you near.

I fear no fate less you so sweet
I fear no world, that remains true
to consume the golden mead
of honest Suns who sing of you.

And this secret, that no one knows
that your shy love has set me free
that deep within my soul you grow
I carry your smile in me.

In me, in me, so deep in me
I carry your smile in me...

With My Eyes

Thus with my very eyes accursed
I stroll from gaudy room to room
extolling song and art and verse
approaching slow beneath the moon.

And with my eyes I see red lace
upon the river of your hair
and swim its length unto your face
the very bloom of joy laid bare.

Then with my eyes engaging yours
we bask inside the sweetest glow
entranced like mythic loves of yore
with only sane restraint our foe.

Alarmed we flee into the eve
unto a bow'r beside the sea.

When Sarah Dreams

When Sarah Dreams, her fears expire
and all her worries fade away
replaced by her own heart's desire
and wishes she has often prayed.

When Sarah dreams, her wants are known
acknowledged by male reverence
where every dance is hers' alone
in royal ballroom radiance.

When Sarah dreams, the stars up high
ignite a chandelier above
and shines a brilliant sapphire light
'pon all that Sarah truly loves.

Asleep, her smile, in deep repose
would challenge Heaven's sweetest rose.

To Know You

To journey the length of your infinite soul.
To scale the peaks of your fey beauty.
To swim the oceans of your haunting eyes.
To breathe the fragrance of your shy smile.
To feel the touch of your soft hands.
To taste the nectar of your sweet lips.
And finally,
To reach The End,
That is all of you.
And collapse,
Enraptured.
Bound within your gentle gaze.
Once and forever,
Revealed.
Freed,
At last,
To know you.

The Locks of Night

From Night I journey ever near
upon a nether tide
with moonlit hours to find your bow'r
and feel you by my side.

My deepest dream, a mystic veil
adorning your sweet face
a star gem crown upon your brow
the aspect of your grace.

I scale dark peaks to find your love
which in the end finds me
and in my smile you rest awhile
a pilgrim in the sea.

I hold you fiercely in the dark
my hands the locks of night
engendering bliss with each soft kiss
until the morning light.

Haunting Me

Remembering your joyous laugh
which flows like liquid golden mead
from gentle tender lips that hath
the thrill of your smile haunting me.

Upon the landscape of my dreams
your vision glows in memory
two jewels rich with knowing gleams
two sad sweet eyes still haunting me.

And echoing The Heavens' grace
your every movement perfectly
enhancing your endearing face
and lovely visage haunting me.

Your beauty in totality
keeps haunting me and haunting me...

Adirondac Eulogy

Anointed on that verdant slope
the maiden lay in sweet repose
'pon dandelion courted grass
where goldthread blossoms lightly dozed.

With mountain daisy braided hair
the breath of sunshine so adorn'd
her crown of silver tresses fair
that crowds of white sweet clover mourn'd.

Knapweed florets share her sleep
and lilies pale her moonlit shroud
with roses as pallbearer blooms
and maple mourners sadly bowed.

Mother Ghost

Dear Mother tell me you have gone
unto a place beloved and pure
please tell me is there life beyond
this mortal realm that I endure.

Oh let me know your spirit thrives
existing on a distant height
and that we truly never die
but are reborn in golden light.

That we continue past the dawn
and shed our fleshen shells goodbye
and fear not dark oblivion
as life advances whence we die.

I pray these words to battle doubt
in humble and most sullen gloom
as every morn your silence shouts
that death is final abject doom.

Three Promises

This granted wish of earthly loss
these ashes spread on verdant cliffs
I grieve 'midst Irish rain and moss
and set my mother's soul adrift.

One golden day--on hilly rise
fair Adirondac lake and tree
with sorrowed song and weeping eye
interred with loving family.

Her last request--my promised fate
yon fallen Gaelic soldiery
my lost great grandfather awaits
at rest beside the Channel Sea.

Alone, alone in Normandy
my ancient father calls to me.

Fusilier

The vaunted Munster Infantry
Thus boarded ship with boot and kit
And 'pon the churlish Channel Sea
Pete Casey steamed to Normandy.

To Normandy! To Normandy!
The Royal Munster Fusiliers
All shouted proud with Gaelic glee
Upon the tossing Channel Sea.

Staunch Irishmen of humble birth
Strong arms and hearts of British rule
Fine lads of freckled wit and mirth
The prideful Munster Dirty Shirts.

Frangalus Clauber kicked their arse
And heralded six months of Hell
Lee Enfield bruised their hands and hearts
And drilled them in the killing arts.

Their home the lonely endless trench
Forboding dank uncovered graves
With wounded sprawled on every bench
All perfumed with a deadman's stench.

Close-quartered drills and night attacks
For weeks without a shower or bath
They scraped their boards of mud and flak
And knitted wire upon their backs.

'Cross fields of muck and smoking death
  Good Sergeant Casey led his boys
  To pay the bloody butcher's debt
  With gun, grenade, and bayonet.

One day a Hun advanced unseen
  A Grenadier still but a lad
  Whose Kugel Ball spit Casey's spleen
  Upon that morn most banefully.

Three days he laid in fevered dreams
  Remembering fair emerald shores
  His wife and children faithfully
  Awaiting him across the sea.

Within a medic's tent he died
Brave Sergeant Casey, Dunchadh Eire!
  Thus buried in French countryside
  Alone beside the Channel tide.

Three days too late for brave Casey
  The Ninth Battalion struck its flag
  Pale remnants of Hell's casualties
  Survivors cursed with memories.

Beyond These Walls

I hear the beating wings of night
the sirens of the sleeping world
I feel the touch of soft starlight
as warm eternity unfurls.

And so I'm bid to leave anon
this humble 'bode of gentle friends
and sighing simple sweet farewells
I bow to life renewed again.

Beyond these walls of flesh I go
unto a realm of peaceful leaves
to float upon a Forest's glow
and bathe in Heaven's tender breeze.

Of Another

And then I saw you were not mine
and that I surely was not yours
and that the heart amour that binds
would rear its joyous face no more.

Your gentle smile endured my need
your laughter haunted all my days
your tender lips will never feed
upon my dark and lonely pain.

I cannot love and worship you
this fevered dream has simply died
with all my hopes and wishes hewed
and nothing left but shameful pride.

Arms of another comfort you
with bitter tears my only due.

Annalee

October breeds a lonely eve
as wounded hearts sublimely bleed
upon this anniversary
of Death embracing Annalee.

This very hour twelve moons ago
my heart was cruelly torn from me
as land's majestic ancient foe
unfairly claimed my Annalee.

Oh God forgive my stupid dare
Forgive our foolish moonlit spree
a soul consumed by dark despair
and endless grief for Annalee.

She took my challenge on that shore
and dove into that shadowed sea
and like an ancient castle door
the water closed on Annalee.

Oh brazen reckless mortal man
oh spawn of stale mortality
left screaming on that horrid sand
forever reft of Annalee.

Each day I drown in Devil's brew
reliving all my fatal deeds
and resurrecting all I rue
my long lost lover Annalee.

Oh Annalee sweet Annalee
each night I waken to my screams
and wander back down to the sea
where I last held my Annalee.

Bright silver waves reflect the moon
and offer up pale hands to me
sweet promise of a gentle doom
uniting me with Annalee.

Cannoneer

Upon this bed I plead my case,
with sad regard and aged breath,
old powder scars upon my face,
this Cannoneer now faces death.

Deserving not my mortal wrath,
and Shaitan's urge to rend and kill,
the unwise souls who crossed my path,
did pay the bloody butcher's bill.

'Gainst many forts in distant lands,
I unleashed thunder on the brave,
As lightning from my leathered hand,
toppled walls and slaughtered knaves.

Among the waves of Mother Sea,
I shot my ball and great ships sank,
and with a fey and evil glee,
I fed the Ocean gore and planks.

Soon my name would thus portend,
a most unholy bloody fuss,
a reputation that I tend,
Mars' terrible own blunderbuss.

In time I earned a Sergeant's stripe,
and healthy fat upon my shank,
until my punishment grew ripe,
and fate attacked my wretched flank.

A freckled lad untried and scared,
overpacked my cannon's bore,
and as the touch-hole belched and flared,
I felt the iron fist of Thor.

Screaming 'neath a medic's saw,
a legless pension for this fiend,
four decades now my sorrow raw,
for all those spirits cannon-cleaved.

My feeble eyes grow faint and dim,
the rumble of artillery near,
"Descend Cur!" Quoth the Reaper's din,
"For final judgement, Cannoneer!"

Aunjanu

Where have you gone my Aunjanu
dark mystery that haunts my soul
and fills my nights with dreams of you
my lovely gentle Aunjanu.

No one has seen you Aunjanu
these many days I sit alone
imagining the art of you
my perfect precious Aunjanu.

They search for you my Aunjanu
in every shed and woodland rise
in lakes and ponds of every hue
my troubled lover Aunjanu.

They think I harmed you Aunjanu
my darling help me prove them wrong
regretting my harsh words to you
come back to me sweet Aunjanu.

Our argument my Aunjanu
which drove you out into the storm
escaping unfair words I slew
I beg forgiveness Aunjanu.

And thus they found me Aunjanu
upon the moors that swallowed you
a wild and fevered ranting fool
bereft of my love Aunjanu.

They come for me now Aunjanu
the clank of rusty metal keys
a mob whose very eyes accuse
and doubt my love for Aunjanu.

And so I stand here Aunjanu
mere moments from a welcome doom
that tears the veil between us two
uniting me with Aunjanu.

Fear

Fear, my Mother fear, my maternal Governess
You hold me tight within the darkness
Too long shielded from all harm
A babe in the wilderness.

Fear, my Father fear, my paternal General
You thrust me onto fields of battle
And cheer me like a Roman
And laugh at my Pyrrhic fall.

Fear, my Sister fear, my sororal Soul
You speak to me of journeys and The Call
And long nights of holy doubt
And see my faith's bitter toll.

Fear, my Brother fear, my fraternal Intellect
You open all the books didactic
And show me paths of wisdom
And find me less than logic.

Fear, my Lover fear, oh my sweet erosal Mate
You share my beds of failure
And you dance inside my hate
You sup upon my native Hells
And sing to me of wraiths
And you alone of all my weirds
Take pleasure in my mortal fate.

All Hallow's Eve

Three nights beyond the Autumn boon
amid the leaf forsaken trees
a rising moon will bleed the rune
and harbinger All Hallow's Eve.

Oh mothers hold your children close
and fathers fall upon your knees
to pray that hosts of monster ghosts
will pass you by All Hallow's Eve.

Then keep the hearth a blazing pyre
for witches fly at night you see
and chimney fires appear too dire
for entry on All Hallow's Eve.

Prepare the scarecrow oh so vile
and jack-o-lantern jubilee
then light the smile that scares awhile
your sentinals All Hallow's Eve.

And finally the offering
of caramel and honeyed sweets
the bribe for things that nighttime brings
placating ghouls All Hallow's Eve.

At last the very night is still
and all are home and safe asleep
bright candles fill each windowsill
protecting you All Hallow's Eve.

Cape's End

Sweet Summer air as thick as dew
gives way to salty scented sighs
and ocean kisses 'pon us few
thus lucky to embrace high tide.

Where travelers take humid hikes
and fishermen haul in their pick
while laughter dodges cars and bikes
on cobblestones and sidewalk brick.

Fair Provincetown you sing to me
far golden land of sand and sails
soft siren call of Sun and sea
is calling me and calling me...

Furnace

Upon a speck of sandy land
on Massachusetts's distant shore
I felt the burn of her soft hand
which seared me to my very core.

Within the oven of my heart
I begged the nature of her taunt
and toured the rhythm of her art
which fueled the engine of my want.

Then 'neath a Summer sun we talked
and walked in crowded narrow streets
devouring cold and creamy draughts
and marveling at window treats.

But afternoons must end it seems
extinguishing my fiery dreams.

Furled Wings

Within a chalky blue serene
at rest beside an azure sea
while drunk on salty spray and heat
an angel sat down next to me.

A visage of both strength and need
a nod of shy complexity
a form of shape and surety
a vision of serenity.

Her laughter draughts of silver wine
with soft fey eyes immensely kind
a smile coquettish and refined
a nature sacred and sublime.

Aloft this sweet mirage a blur
thus left this wretched Earthbound cur.

Harbor Night

An evening tryst through shadowed door
upon a path of sand and shells
we stroll along the harbor shore
and watch white sails depart the swells.

Then in the streets the laughing streets
the bright parade and majesty
of youth and strength and fevered feet
revives our souls and sets us free.

Enfolding us this humid hug
of neon light and party bar
alluring naughty Neptune's drug
we kiss and sway beneath the stars.

Wet joyous thrill born of the sea
sweet echo of eternity.

Is Still

And for one moment thus appeared
'fore sullen sky and furled sail
outlined in nature's very tears
a vision cowled in silver veil.

A miracle so timely feigned
this fantasy of sultry grace
that jagged shards of golden bane
eclipsed her effervescent face.

My heart is still upon that shore
that lovely inner harbor beach
that stage for all that I adore
and dream I can no longer reach.

Provincetown

In Provincetown I floated on
the tender breath of ocean breeze
down narrow streets of shops anon
all perfumed by the open Sea.

A joyous roof of blue and white
a ragtag fleet of gaudy sails
a postcard etched in golden light
the breach and spray of humpbacked whales.

The laughter of a Summer day
piled ice cream cones and paper fans
tough weathered fishermen at bay
the musky smell of catch at hand.

Kaleidoscopic majesty
symphonic raucous harbored glee.

Remember Thee

Your dancing eyes like precious jewels
reflecting joyful inner glee
so fill my heart with sweet renewal
thus I would pray remember thee.

Your soul which mirrors heaven's gaze
would fill an artist's gallery
of precious smile and loving face
thus I would pray remember thee.

Then decades whence my vision dims
while resting by the open sea
I'll dream we kissed upon a whim
thus I would pray remember thee.

And in one thousand years or more this fragment
of pale gallantry
will manifest your charming grace and all will
pray remember thee.

Autumn

Autumn breathes a magic sigh
exhaling golden amber leaves
and freshly bubbling apple pies
and maple farmers tapping trees.

Sweet cider strengthens every arm
as raking armies take the field
reclaiming conquered grassy yards
while Autumn mothers spice their meals.

Autumn evenings come to life
with pumpkin cookies soft and warm
while all the naughty children hide
refusing meals of squash and corn.

The fireplace is finally lit
by Autumn fathers coughing loud
and smores are toasted while they sit
on woolen blankets spread around.

And at the end of Autumn days
October moons with orange grins
enchant us with their tender gaze
until we fall asleep again.

Autumn Stroll

Beneath a sleeping canopy
soft luminescent fingers search
and dapple 'pon both twig and leaf
like golden freckles on the earth.

Autumn Blush

And in my dream I journey forth
in search of golden amber leaves
unto a wondrous realm up north
of vibrant Adirondac trees.

Towering giants guard their home
tall sentinels with silver crowns
aged warriors hewn from stone
eternal soldiers standing proud.

I sail the rolling highway lanes
and breath sweet air as thick as mead
and taste the music of the rain
amidst this vast chromatic sea.

Thus Summer fades upon a hush
releasing Autumn's tender blush.

Grave Troopers

Thus morning spilled upon the rank
and file of yellow, red, and green
encamped on ancient riverbanks
brave staggered rows of orchard trees.

A harvest war their looming fate
upon the morning bugle call
barbarians with wicker crates
attack with mindless hungry gall.

Yon valiant doomed defense is drawn
'round crusty spiny warriors
soon overwhelmed and slain upon
this battlefield of apple gore.

At dusk the massacre abates
and orphaned seeds renew their fate.

November Dreams

November's sky is soft and grey
and silver lines its supple seams
which cover fields of rollen hay
and slowly swaying drowsy trees.

November's breath provides a shade
for secret and romantic trysts
and whispers that a shorter day
engenders longer nighttime bliss.

September and October days
will claim the fading Summer gleam
yet standing tall to Winter's gaze
are all of my November dreams.

November

Morning frost reveals her face
which spurs a Robin's breast to sing
that with serene and subtle grace
November comes awandering.

Suburban lawns have shed their leaves
while silos have filled up with corn
and summer camps sleep quietly
while empty beaches sit forlorn.

November clouds are thick and full
of promises and pale renewal
impatient 'til the Autumn lull
expires in Winter's rain of jewels.

Then closet raiders excavate
thick musty coats exhumed and worn
while scarves and gloves resuscitate
old fashions that are soon reborn.

November eves rush to the door
as Mothers cook up warming meals
and athletes come home cold and sore
to sit before the hearth and heal.

Beneath November's starry guise
cold Dads invade the attic trunks
to liberate a woolen prize
of blankets piled upon the bunks.

And buried in a fluffy heap
and laying there all safe and warm
November whispers pleasant sleep
until the early break of morn.

Winter Tears

The ending of a long embrace
as pale white arms retreat from sight
and expectation fills a space
from whence this siren spent the night.

Her gossamer and flowing gown
long strewn for months across the land
is yanked from off the startled ground
and slipp'd o'er two supple hands.

Then fleeing North to her abode
across the dampened virgin ponds
so newly birthed of mountain snow
reflecting all the fires of dawn.

That all her crystal paramours
and courtiers of chiller days
now spill their lives upon the floor
a flood of saddened April pain.

Frail icicles shrug off the perch
and leap to join their fallen peers
as fields of sleepers feel the lurch
and wake to drink these Winter tears.

Winter Bride

The silence of a gentle prayer
the beauty of a silver veil
a breath of waking frosty air
a smiling kiss of softest pale.

Reveals the early blush of dawn
well mirrored in her eyes adorned
with dancing rainbow motes anon
a lush kaleidoscope reborn.

And as prismatic crowds abide
the Sun itself ascends the land
to gaze upon his wedding bride
fair Winter who now takes his hand.

Ice Maiden

Each white and frosty year you're born
to stand within the Winter Faire
beneath a silver sun adorned
with rainbows in your sparkling hair.

Admired by each passing boy
and envied by shy pouting girls
perfection in your frozen joy
and grace in every cut and curl.

A tainted Knight and caring not
ignoring every sneer and barb
I guard your virtue in this lot
sweet princess of the shining garb.

And I alone express the pain
of unrequited passion's sting
and keep a vigil free of shame
which warm desire always brings.

Until old Winter starts to wane
and fading like a silent song
you leave me all alone again
to sadly ponder where you've gone.

April's Reign

Warm winds wake the forests
fair flowers dot the plains
kisses 'pon new green'ry
oh witness April's reign.

Crystal slumbers ending
an ocean pale recedes
falling nature's nectar
unto the thirsty seed.

Shout out to this season
wet breath of life that sings
snowflakes favor Winter
but raindrops worship Spring!

Spring

Long underwear and woolen shirts
are newly shed to welcome Spring
while stirring beneath Winter's skirts
the air unflutters honeyed wings.

April breakfast greets the child
whose smile betrays a sudden zeal
as melons, eggs, and orange juice
replace five months of hot oatmeal.

And down beneath the rising sun
across the bark of wrinkled trees
the freckled green of sprouting buds
announce the birth of stalks and leaves.

Gritting teeth and bruising legs
as arms of buckets knock his knees
the maple farmer hammers pegs
the prize and pain of tapping trees.

Loud children of most every age
soon race around the damp outdoors
and mothers scream in shrill outrage
as virgin mud is tracked on floors.

Umbrellas bloom across all streets
as laughing rain and puddles dance
the splash that sets one's heart to beat
the spray that spurs the young to prance.

And as Spring evenings reach their close
the sun prolongs its slow retreat
reluctant to begin its doze
regretting Winter's reign of sleep.

Summertime

To wax the day in decadence
reclined upon a beach sublime
beneath a palette blue and white
a dream in lazy summertime.

And thundering over grassy dunes
a sweet excess of limber thighs
engulfed by youth's adrenaline
a dream in breezy summertime.

To splash at last in mother sea
naive and deaf to Autumn's chime
enrapt with nature's vibrant bath
a dream in hazy summertime.

Afloat in glowing amber climes
and golden waves of summertime.

Summer's Breath

A gossamer and golden sigh
a tender honeysuckle kiss
the shimmer of a red sunrise
the warmth of sultry nighttime bliss.

Flows out anew across the land
embracing spirits young and old
saffronic shifts of whispering sand
bright banes to Winter's reign of cold.

Until the very Earth exhales
and voids the pain 'tween life and death
confounding Spring and Autumn's pale
consumed in Summer's fiery breath.

And cast 'neath burning amber skies
The fevered lust of feral eyes.

Precious Petals

Softly slowly falling tears
August's grief a rain of red
scattered smiles and fading fears
scales of Summer dragons dead.

Honey moist a cooling breeze
sumptuous seas of golden fruit
valleys rich with verdant leaves
luscious kingdoms ripe to loot.

Angel feathers smooth and light
blanketing sweet lovely loam
silken wings of ruby night
precious petals all alone.

Thus Summer bowed its weary head
as each and every flower bled.

Sirens

Nine sirens who have haunted me
upon an electronic shore
since start of this young century
inspiring my humble lore.

Fair Jaime's arch Missouri zeal
tough Cassie's Texan spirit soars
Kim's Netherlandish brash appeal
fab Fabienne's Brit laughter roars.

Sweet Lee Ann's cyber canvas gleams
Canadian's nordique amour
Karima dancing desert dreams
Lei of Pacific green outdoors.

With Sarah's poise and charms and arts
They heal my soul, and steal my heart.